What's in This Book

Do you ever wonder what makes you grow? Or why you shiver when you are cold? Have you ever marveled at the speed of a cheetah, the fastest land animal on Earth? Or been awed at how a chameleon can change color? Solving such mysteries is part and parcel of animal physiology, the science that investigates how different animal bodies work. Learning how they do so increases our appreciation of the uniqueness and diversity of the vast animal kingdom, and adds to our understanding of how our own bodies work. *How Bodies Work: Animal Physiology* offers a glimpse inside ourselves and the amazing creatures around us.

The COME LEARN WITH ME series encourages children's natural curiosity about the world by introducing them to exciting areas in science. Each book deals with a specific topic, and can be read alone or together with an adult. With lively, reader-friendly texts and numerous engaging illustrations, the books will entertain and inform children and adults alike. No previous knowledge of the subject is needed. Scientific vocabulary appears in **bold type** and is defined in context, but is also listed in the Glossary at the end of the book. Let these books be your guide as you enter the fascinating world of science, where you are sure to discover many new interests and vastly expand your horizons.

COME
LEARN WITH ME

How Bodies Work: Animal Physiology

Text by Bridget Anderson

BANK STREET COLLEGE OF EDUCATION
in association with the
AMERICAN MUSEUM OF NATURAL HISTORY
for Lickle Publishing Inc

First published in 2003 by
LICKLE PUBLISHING INC

Library of Congress Control Number
2002113575
ISBN: 1-890674-16-8

ILLUSTRATION AND PHOTO CREDITS
ACT, Cathedral Church of St. John the Divine 11b, 19b, 44, 45tr; American Museum of Natural History 7t,7c, 9bl, 12br, 13tr, 13br, 14t, 14c, 15tr, 15c, 15br, 18t, 18bl, 18br, 19cr, 20t, 20-21b, 21cr, 22tr, 23tr, 24t, 24b, 25tl, 25tr, 25b, 26t, 27cr, 27tr, 28c, 30t, 31br, 33tl, 33cl, 33bl, 33tr, 36b, 37tr, 38tr, 38cl, 38b, 40c, 40b, 41tr, 41c—AMNH photographers J. Beckett/C. Chesek 14b; A.J. Emmerich 45; C.H. Greenwalt 6b; B.J. Kaston 30b, 45tl; J. Knull 3; G. Lower 7b; Frank Puza 42c; J.E. Thompson 17c—; Dee Breger, Lamont-Doherty Earth Observatory 9tl, 9tr, 40b; Caribbean Conservation Corporation 39tr; Charles Davey 41br; Michael Davidson, Molecular Expressions 10t, 10b; Wim van Egmond 2-3, 8bl, 8br, 26cl; Warren Finke 35tl; Grant Gentry 23br; Elizabeth Gibbs 12t, 43b; Keith F. Goodnight, Southern Methodist University 23bl; Pamela J. W. Gore, Georgia Perimeter College 23tl; William Hahn, Department of Ecology, Evolution, and Environmental Biology, Center for Environmental Research and Conservation, Columbia University 22; Mick Hoult 42b; Cait Hutnik 12bl; Jim Kalish, University of Nebraska-Lincoln, Department of Entomology 17tr; John Kane 2, 6t; LifeART image copyright 2002 Lippincott Williams & Wilkins. All rights reserved. 28, 29t, 29b, 31t, 37t, 43br. Thanks to USC Department of Cardiothoracic Surgery (www.cts.usc.edu) for assistance; Naomi F. Miller 34tr; NASA 16c; National Heart, Lung, and Blood Institute 35tr; National Institute on Drug Abuse 16t; National Ocean Service Photo Gallery 34cr; National Oceanic and Atmospheric Administration (NOAA) Photo Library 27b, 31b—NOAA photographer Mary Hollinger 17tl; Torquay International School, Ltd. 13bl; USDA 11t, 34c, 42t; USGS: Nelson Beyer 1, 43tl, 43c; Damien Ossi 43cl; Sherrie Wick 8tr, 8cr, 8r; Illustrations: Nancy Heim 32, 35bl, 35br, 39tl, 39b, 41bl

Series producer: Charles Davey LLC, New York
Text edited by Bank Street College of Education:
Andrea Perelman, Project Manager; Elisabeth Jakab, Project Editor
Photographs unless otherwise credited from the American Museum of Natural History:
Maron L. Waxman, Editorial Director; Eric Brothers, Scientific Consultant
Art Direction, Production, & Design: Charles Davey *design* LLC
Photo research: Erin Barnett

Printed in China

CONTENTS

The Miracle of Life   6-7

The Building Blocks of Bodies   8-9

Where Animals Get Their Energy   10-11

The Regulation of Bodies   12-13

Skeletons and Muscles   14-15

The Nervous System   16-17

The Human Nervous System   18-19

The Endocrine System   20-21

The Respiratory System   22-23

The Human Respiratory System   24-25

The Circulatory System   26-27

The Human Heart   28-29

The Digestive System   30-31

The Human Digestive System   32-33

The Excretory System   34-35

The Human Urinary System   36-37

The Immune System   38-39

The Human Immune System   40-41

Creating New Life   42-43

The Body is a Finely-Tuned Machine   44-45

Glossary   46-47

Index   48

The Miracle of Life

Have you ever wondered what makes you grow? Why you shiver when you are cold? Or how your body makes you laugh or cry?

Have you ever marveled at how a caterpillar turns into a butterfly, how a cheetah can run so fast, or how a chameleon changes the color of its body to match its background?

Dancers from the Pilobolus Dance Theater show off the beauty and flexibility of the human body.

Hummingbirds must eat three to five times every hour. They have thin beaks and long tongues—perfect for licking the nectar from flowers.

Animals do such amazing things because they are living beings that can respond to the world around them in different ways. They are able to move, grow, repair themselves, and create new life. Some animals, including humans, can also learn and remember.

Most animals function efficiently in their home environment. Their bodies are **adapted** to the conditions in their habitat, whether they have thick fur for life on a snowy mountainside or gills to breathe water in the deep ocean. Whatever the location, each animal develops and maintains a fine coordination among the different parts of its body in order to survive where it lives.

Mountain goats have thick hair and produce a lot of body heat, enabling them to survive in the cold Alaskan mountains.

Beavers gnaw on trees with their strong teeth to get wood for building their lodges.

Many people have spent their lives trying to understand just how the bodies of animals work. This area of study is called **animal physiology**.

Humans are among the most complex of all animals. If you could look inside your own body, you'd see that it is packed full of interconnected parts that fit together efficiently inside your skin. All bodies, yours and those of all other animals, are beautiful, dynamic living organisms.

The squid's excellent eyesight allows it to see in deep, dark ocean water.

The Building Blocks of Bodies

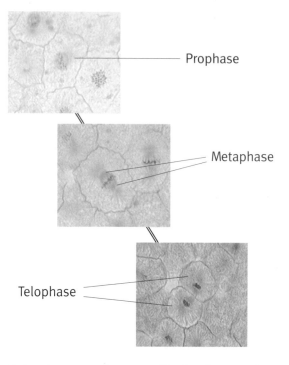

Prophase

Metaphase

Telophase

Scientists can observe cells dividing under a microscope. Top: the center cell is getting ready to divide (known as prophase). Middle: the cell's materials are separating and moving to opposite sides (known as metaphase). Bottom: the cell is pinching off into two separate cells (known as telophase).

Animals' bodies consist of many different parts, each with a special job. All the parts work together to carry out the necessary activities that enable an animal to function.

Think of an animal's body as being like a sand castle made of tiny grains of sand. Similarly, animals are made of tiny building blocks called **cells**. The larger the animal, the more cells it has. To make a sand castle bigger, you add more sand. An animal gets bigger by creating more cells. Cells are alive, and as an animal lives and grows, the cells in its body divide to make new cells.

Skin cells have a flat and wide shape.

The cells in most animals are not all alike. Cells have different sizes and shapes depending on the work they do. Flat, wide skin cells cover and protect the body. Muscle cells are fibrous,

that is, made of long, slender pieces. They can lengthen and shorten themselves to help an animal move. Brain cells are long and narrow and send out branches that make contact with other brain cells.

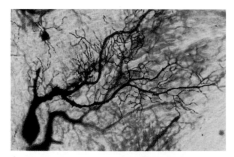

Brain cells, called neurons, have many branches. Notice how the branches of these two neurons connect with each other.

Your heart is a muscle that does not get tired the way your arm and leg muscles do. Notice the long fibers of the heart's muscle tissue.

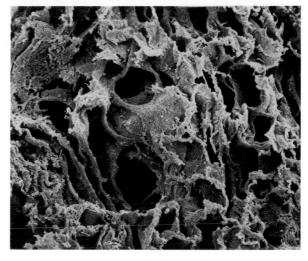

Lung tissue is full of holes that fill with air when you breathe.

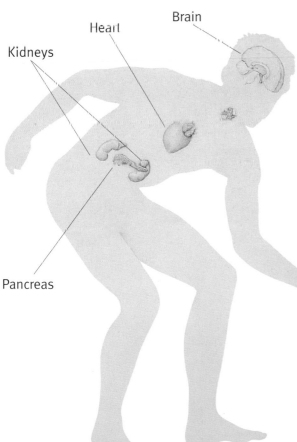

Brain

Heart

Kidneys

Pancreas

Groups of the same kind of cells join together to make **tissue**. Muscles are tissues made from muscle cells. Skin tissue is made from skin cells. Certain tissues come together to form **organs**. Organs, such as the heart, lungs, kidneys, and liver, do the work of the body. An animal's entire skin is considered an organ, too. It covers and protects everything inside the body.

Groups of organs and tissues are linked together in systems to carry out certain tasks, such as breathing or digesting food. These organ systems all work together to keep an animal alive and healthy.

Most of the organs in your body, including the brain, heart, kidneys, and pancreas, are located in your head, chest, and abdomen.

Where Animals Get Their Energy

Animals need a constant supply of energy to move, grow, and carry out all their activities. Where does that energy come from? It is made in the cells— the animal's energy factories.

Food, water, and oxygen are converted to energy, chemicals, and other useful materials inside your cells. When you eat, drink, and breathe, you are actually feeding the billions of cells that make up your body. When you feel hungry, it is really your cells that are hungry. When you feel thirsty, your cells need more water.

Animal Cell

An animal cell has many different organelles, including lysosomes, mitochondria, and a nucleus. The organelles sit in the cell's cytoplasm, which is surrounded by a cell membrane.

Cell Membrane

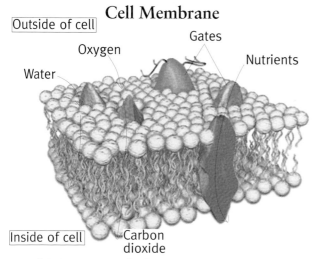

This is a magnified section of a cell membrane. Water, oxygen, and carbon dioxide gases are small enough to slip through the membrane. Larger particles, such as nutrients, have to travel through the membrane's gates.

Nutrients are the substances in food that cells use to do their work. Each type of nutrient has a special job. **Carbohydrates** are the main fuel that cells use to make energy. **Protein** provides the building materials to make muscles, bones, teeth, hair, and other body structures. **Fat** is a second kind of fuel. If the body does not have enough carbohydrates, cells will "burn" fat to make energy. **Vitamins** and **minerals** help make certain chemicals and structures in the body and assist in repairing injuries.

To get all the nutrients your body needs, you must eat a variety of foods. The US Food and Drug Administration created this food pyramid as a guideline for healthy eating.

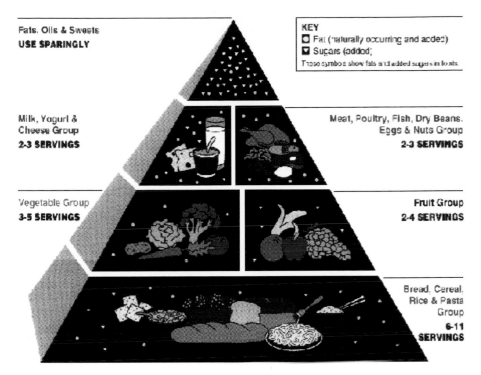

Fats, Oils & Sweets
USE SPARINGLY

KEY
☐ Fat (naturally occurring and added)
◼ Sugars (added)
These symbols show fats and added sugars in foods.

Milk, Yogurt & Cheese Group
2-3 SERVINGS

Meat, Poultry, Fish, Dry Beans, Eggs & Nuts Group
2-3 SERVINGS

Vegetable Group
3-5 SERVINGS

Fruit Group
2-4 SERVINGS

Bread, Cereal, Rice & Pasta Group
6-11 SERVINGS

Just as organs do the work of the body, each cell contains **organelles** ("little organs") that do the work of the cell. For example, the **nucleus**, the cell's "brain," directs the cell's activities. **Lysosomes** process nutrients. **Mitochondria** convert water, oxygen, and nutrients into energy.

Organelles are suspended in a jelly-like substance called **cytoplasm**. The cytoplasm is surrounded by a thin covering, called the **cell membrane**.

A cell's membrane has tiny holes for water and oxygen to pass through. However, nutrients and most other materials have to pass through special "gates." These gates are the security guards of the cell and protect it from harmful bacteria and viruses that might make an animal sick. Waste from cells, including carbon dioxide and unused nutrients, leaves the cell through the membrane as well.

A healthy diet gives you strength and energy.

The Regulation of Bodies

Homeostasis

An animal must keep the environment *inside* its body comfortable for its cells and organs, no matter how the environment *outside* its body changes. Cells can do their jobs only if their conditions stay fairly constant. If the inside environment gets too hot or too cold, or too wet or too dry, the cells can't work properly. They also need a continuous supply of nutrients, water, and oxygen, the right amount of salt, and a way to get rid of wastes. The ability of animals to do these things— to regulate the internal environment of their bodies— is called **homeostasis**.

Dogs pant to cool their bodies.

The body has ways of telling an animal what it needs and what to do to satisfy those needs. For example, if the inside of an animal is dehydrated (too dry), the animal will become thirsty and drink. Likewise, if the body needs more nutrients, the animal will become hungry and look for something to eat.

Because they need water to survive, wildebeest migrate each year during the dry season to find water sources.

A desert snake's thick skin helps it to retain moisture.

12

Musk oxen can survive in cold Arctic climates because they are endothermic animals— their bodies produce heat.

Usually, your body maintains homeostasis without your having to think about it. Think about your body temperature. If you are cold, you automatically start to shiver— a shaking muscle movement that speeds the flow of blood and warms

Turning on an air conditioner is a behavioral action that can help your body cool down.

you up. If you are hot, you naturally sweat. That is, your skin produces moisture that cools you down as it evaporates.

Sweating and shivering are called physiological actions— they occur inside the body. But if you can't get warm enough by shivering, you might put on a sweater.

If sheep cannot cool themselves by sweating, they move into the shade.

If you can't cool down enough by sweating, you might turn on a fan or air conditioner. These are behavioral actions. They also help maintain homeostasis.

Endothermic ("inside heat") animals, mostly mammals and birds, can regulate their body temperature physiologically and behaviorally. **Ectothermic** ("outside heat") animals, which include most other animals, have to rely on behavioral actions alone. For example, a desert toad needs to find a sunny spot to warm up, or a shady one to cool down.

Because its body cannot produce heat, a desert toad warms its ectothermic body on a sunny rock.

13

Skeletons and Muscles

The Structure and Movement of Animals

A land snail grows a shell that protects its soft body.

A sand castle quickly dissolves into a pile of sand if disturbed by a wave or the wind. What keeps an animal's body from dissolving into a pile of cells? Its tissues are strong and hold the body together. Many animals also have a **skeleton** that gives their bodies structure and protects their organs.

Some animals have skeletons made from sturdy bone material inside their bodies. These animals are called **vertebrates**. (Each bone in your backbone is known as a vertebra.)

A sea star's skeleton is its spiny skin!

Most animals do not have bones. They are called **invertebrates** (without backbones). Some do have a skeleton, but it is on the outside of their bodies, like armor. One kind of armor is called an **exoskeleton** ("exo" means outside). Exoskeletons give animals such as insects and millipedes their shape, structure, and protection.

Other invertebrates have no skeleton. Some, such as clams and snails, grow a shell to hide inside, but others, such as worms and slugs, have no hard structure to protect their bodies.

Some animals grow segmented exoskeletons. See if you can find the ant, millipede, and daddy longlegs in this museum diorama.

Because humans are vertebrates, you have bones that extend through your back, legs, arms, fingers, and toes. Your bony rib cage surrounds your heart and lungs. Your brain is safely housed inside your hard, bony skull.

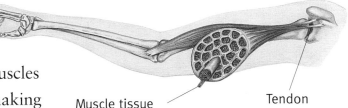

If you could look under your skin, you would see a skeleton of bones covered by muscles.

This penguin skeleton clearly shows the animal's body plan including its beak, wings, and tail.

Most animals move by using **muscles**, tissue that can lengthen and shorten. In vertebrates, strong connective tissue called **ligaments** hold bones together, and **tendons** attach muscles to bones. When muscles shorten, they pull on the bones, making them move. When you bend your arm, the muscles on the front side of your elbow shorten, pulling your lower arm bone closer to your upper arm. At the

Arm Muscle

Each muscle in your body is made up of bundles of muscle tissues which are connected to bones by tendons.

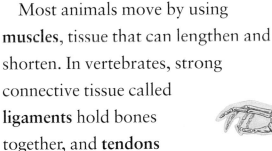

Muscle tissue

Tendon

same time, the muscles on the back of your elbow stretch, allowing your arm to bend.

The Nervous System
Command Central

The command center for an animal's body is its **nervous system**. This system directs an animal's activities and guides how an animal reacts to its environment. One of the most important functions of the nervous system is to control homeostasis. It is in charge of both the physiological actions (heart rate, breathing, shivering) and the behavioral actions (eating, drinking, moving) of the body.

Nervous systems are made up of cells called neurons, which carry messages to and from different parts of the body to

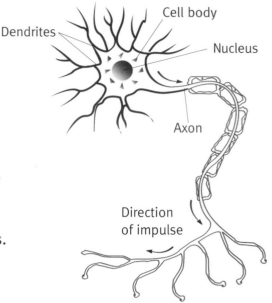

Structure of a Neuron

A neuron has a number of branches that extend from the main cell body. Dendrites are the branches that receive impulses from other cells. The axon is the branch that sends impulses to other cells. When a neuron receives an impulse through its dendrites, the impulse travels through the cell body and down the axon.

You can imagine a nervous system as the "control tower" of a body—overseeing and directing activity.

tell it what to do. Neurons send bits of electricity, called impulses, from one neuron to the next. In most animals, groups of neurons join together in long bundles called **nerves**. Nerves are like information "highways" for the messages being sent and received through impulses.

A sponge is one of the simplest kinds of animals. It does not have a nervous system.

Grasshopper Nervous System

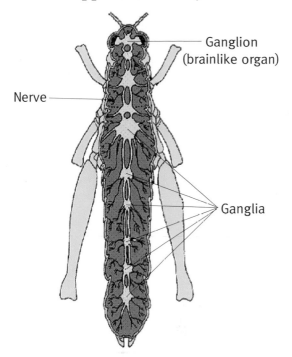

Ganglion (brainlike organ)

Nerve

Ganglia

Nerves branch through a grasshopper's body. Its nervous system is controlled by ganglia in the head and along the nerve cord.

More active animals tend to have more complex nervous systems. A sponge anchored to the seafloor is one of the least active animals. It has no nervous system at all, though it can react to its environment in simple ways. A jellyfish floating in the ocean has a loose web of neurons called a **nerve net** that extends through its body. When one neuron is stimulated, it sends impulses through the whole nerve net, making the entire body react. For example, if a jellyfish senses something nearby, the nerve net responds by directing the body to make swimming motions toward potential food or away from danger.

A jellyfish has a simple nervous system called a nerve net.

In the bodies of flying insects and slithering worms, groups of neurons gather together in simple brainlike organs called **ganglia** (singular: ganglion). From these organs, thick nerves called **nerve cords** extend through the center of the body. Smaller and smaller nerves branch off from the nerve cords to reach all areas of the body.

The Human Nervous System

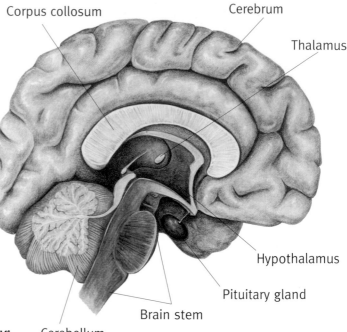

Corpus collosum

Cerebrum

Thalamus

Hypothalamus

Pituitary gland

Brain stem

Cerebellum

Vertebrates and other complex animals have a nervous system controlled by a **brain,** a gray, wrinkly organ made up millions of neurons. The brain connects to a vast network of nerves and other organs that coordinate the body's activities.

You could not survive without your brain. It processes information and directs the body's actions. It tells the heart to beat, lungs to breathe, and muscles to move. It reacts to information from the world outside through your ears, eyes, nose, mouth, and skin. It also controls the homeostasis of your body.

There are many different regions on your brain. Each region controls specific activities. If you cut a human brain down the middle, you would see the brain stem (red); cerebellum (dark yellow); hypothalamus, thalamus, and pituitary gland (purple); the corpus collosum (bright yellow); and the cerebral cortex (blue).

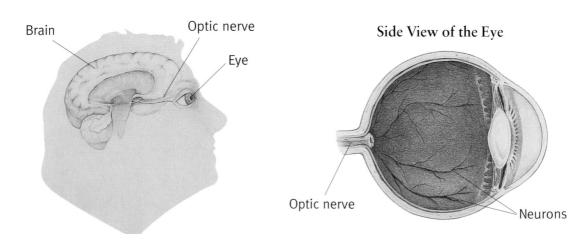

Brain

Optic nerve

Eye

Side View of the Eye

Optic nerve

Neurons

An optic nerve connects each eye to the brain. The eye receives information in its neurons and sends that information through the optic nerve to the brain.

Here is how the human nervous system works: The **spinal cord**, a thick bundle of nerves running down your back, links your brain to the rest of your body. The brain and spinal cord use two kinds of neurons to communicate with the body. **Sensory neurons** gather information from all parts of the body and carry it to the brain and spinal cord. **Motor neurons** deliver orders from the brain and spinal cord telling the body what to do and how to respond to information provided by the sensory neurons.

Different regions of the brain control specific activities in the body. Hearing, seeing, smelling, tasting, and talking, are each controlled by separate regions. One area coordinates your movements. Another controls your emotions— you cry when this area directs your body to create tears. You laugh when it creates a special brain chemical to make you feel happy.

Certain regions of your brain are unconscious— that is, they are always on "autopilot." They direct activities in your body, such as breathing, digestion, and creating new cells, without any thought from you. Learning, memory, and thinking are controlled by conscious parts of your brain.

Brain

Spinal chord

Nerves

The human nervous system is an intricate network of nerves controlled by the brain and spinal cord.

If you think something is funny, your brain tells you to laugh.

The Endocrine System

The Body's Chemical Messenger

Pituitary gland

Thyroid and parathyroid glands

Thymus gland

Adrenal glands

Pancreas

The glands of the endocrine system are located on or near major organs in the body.

The **endocrine system** acts as the brain's assistant. It sends substances with chemical messages from the brain, telling the body what to do to maintain homeostasis, how to grow and develop, when to reproduce, and how to deal with stress.

These chemical substances are called **hormones**. There are many kinds, and each carries specific instructions. One hormone tells an animal it needs to eat more. Another tells it when to sleep.

The word "hormone" comes from the Greek word *hormon*, which means "to excite." Hormones can stimulate, or excite, an animal's body to do amazing things. They instruct a caterpillar how and when to change its body into a moth or butterfly, and they tell a chameleon to change its body color to match its background. In humans, they let your body know when to grow and how to develop.

Hormones are produced in special organs, called **glands**, found throughout the body. Each gland stores its hormones until the nervous system instructs it to send them as a message. For example, when an animal becomes scared or excited, the brain tells the adrenal gland to send the hormone

A cheetah produces adrenaline when it chases its prey. The prey, an antelope in this case, produces adrenaline as it tries to run away.

Two hormones, insulin and glucagon, help to maintain the homeostasis of a body's blood sugar. If there is too much sugar in the blood— after eating ice cream, for instance— insulin tells the body to store the extra sugar for later. If there is not enough sugar in the blood, glucagon tells the body to take stored sugar and return it to the blood.

adrenaline through the body. Adrenaline is called the "fight or flight" hormone. It prepares an animal's body to run away from danger, fight for survival, or handle other stressful situations. When a cheetah chases an antelope, both animals use adrenaline. Adrenaline helps the antelope flee from danger and the cheetah to catch the food it needs to survive. When you are nervous or excited— on a roller-coaster ride for example— adrenaline makes your heart beat faster.

Hormones in a caterpillar's body tell it when to create a cocoon and how to change its body into a moth.

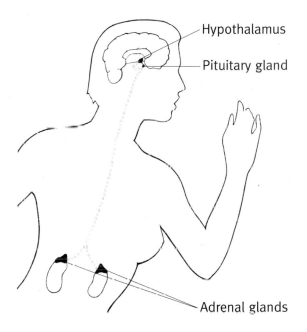

- Hypothalamus
- Pituitary gland
- Adrenal glands

The adrenal gland produces adrenaline. When the body needs adrenaline, the hypothalamus region of the brain sends a message to the pituitary gland. Then, the pituitary gland tells the adrenal gland to make adrenaline.

The Respiratory System

Oxygen In; Carbon Dioxide Out

Flatworms called planaria have such tiny, thin bodies that their cells can absorb oxygen directly from the environment.

Most animals cannot survive without a constant supply of **oxygen**. If your cells are without it for even a few minutes, they— and you— start to die. That is why you never stop breathing, even when you sleep.

Oxygen is a gas found in both air and water. Animals living in lakes, rivers, and oceans get oxygen by breathing water, and animals living on land get it by breathing air. Breathing is also the way animals get rid of **carbon dioxide**, a gas which cells produce as waste. Animals regulate their breathing to maintain homeostasis. For example, they breathe faster and deeper when exercising because the cells need more oxygen. They breathe slower and shallower when sleeping because less oxygen is needed.

Background image: Plants and algae produce the oxygen that animals need.

In tiny animals like flatworms, most cells are in direct contact with the outside environment. That means oxygen and carbon dioxide can pass freely between the cells and the air or water. In larger or more complex animals, most cells are inside their bodies. Only the surface cells can get oxygen directly from the air or water. These animals have **respiratory systems** to transport oxygen and carbon dioxide between the outside environment and their inner cells.

A sponge breathes water through pores in its body.

Gills

Like all fish, the sling-jawed wrasse gets oxygen from the water, through gills on the sides of its head.

Insects have body openings called **spiracles** to let in oxygen. Air enters the spiracles and flows through a network of branching tubes called **tracheae** (singular: trachea). Oxygen passes through the tubes' walls and into the inner cells through their membranes. Carbon dioxide passes out of the cells and exits the body through the same tubes. Insects continually pump fresh air into their spiracles by expanding and contracting their bodies. Similarly, sponges take in water through small holes called **pores**, which lead to a system of tubes that reach all the cells.

Many animals, including humans, have special organs to pump oxygen into the body. Aquatic animals, such as fish, have **gills**, and land animals, such as humans, have **lungs**.

The orange spots on this caterpillar are its spiracles, the openings through which insects breathe.

spiracles

Spiracles   Trachea

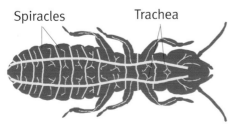

The spiracles on an insect's body lead to a system of branching tubes called trachea that bring oxygen to all the cells.

23

The Human Respiratory System

To blow up a balloon, sing a song, or chase a butterfly, humans rely on the help of their lungs.

Your lungs sit inside your rib cage. They expand as they fill with air and contract as they expel it. The movement of your **diaphragm**, a large, dome-shaped muscle under your lungs, helps you breathe. This muscle pulls downward to create the extra space the lungs need to expand and fill with air. Then the diaphragm relaxes and moves back up, shoving the air out of the lungs and making them smaller again.

Nose

Mouth

Trachea

Lungs

Diaphragm

When you breathe in through your nose and mouth, your diaphragm pulls down, allowing your lungs to expand as they fill with air.

Because they have strong lungs, timber wolves can run for miles without having to stop and rest.

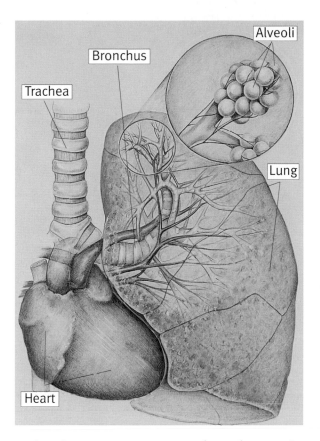

Trachea
Bronchus
Alveoli
Lung
Heart

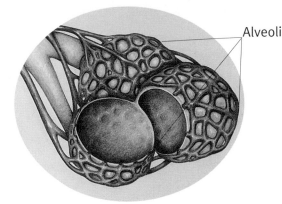

Alveoli

When you inhale, air flows down your trachea into your bronchi and through smaller and smaller tubes in the lungs. Eventually the air reaches the tiny alveoli. Blood which has circulated through the body (blue) is pumped from the heart into the lungs. There the blood picks up oxygen and drops off carbon dioxide in the alveoli. Once the blood is full of oxygen (red), it travels back to the heart to be pumped throughout the body.

As air enters your mouth and nose, it goes down a tube called the **trachea**, or windpipe. Inside your rib cage, the trachea splits into two tubes called **bronchi**— one for each lung. These branch into smaller and smaller tubes, filling all parts of the lung with air. At their very ends are thin air sacs called **alveoli** that look like tiny bunches of grapes. Oxygen passes though these sacs and catches a ride to all parts of the body in the bloodstream, the main liquid transportation system of the body. Red blood cells take oxygen from the alveoli and drop off carbon dioxide picked up from the cells. When you exhale, you push out unused air and carbon dioxide through the same tubes the oxygen used to come in.

Some animals are efficient breathers. They take in a lot of oxygen each time they inhale. A wolf can run for miles without having to stop and "catch its breath." Other animals are less efficient. The lion, although fast, gets easily "out of breath" because its body does not take in enough oxygen with each breath to maintain its pace for long.

Lions run fast to catch their prey, but their lungs tire quickly.

25

The Circulatory System

An Animal's Internal Transportation System

A clam has an open circulatory system. Its cells are directly bathed in blood.

Your family might use a car to pick up groceries. A garbage truck takes your trash to the dump. An ambulance rushes medical professionals to the site of an emergency. Animals bodies also have ways to transport materials, such as oxygen, nutrients, hormone messages, and waste to different body parts.

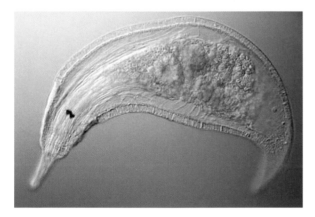

Flatworms stretch and scrunch their bodies in order to move materials from cell to cell.

Flatworms and other simple animals stretch and scrunch their bodies to move materials between neighboring cells. Larger animals have a **circulatory system** in which substances catch a ride to all body parts in a fluid called **blood**. Blood circulates (moves) through the body and acts as grocery getter, garbage picker-upper, and ambulance all in one. Special pumping organs, such as hearts and gills, keep the blood continually moving.

Some animals, including insects and clams, have "open" circulatory systems. Blood washes directly over their organs, passing fresh materials into the cells and carrying away waste materials. Their pumping organs fill with blood and then push it back into the body by contracting (squeezing).

Other animals, including earthworms, sea stars, octopuses, and all vertebrates, have "closed" circulatory systems because the blood does not flow freely through the body.

Instead, it is channeled through a series of tubes called **blood vessels.** The **heart** pumps "fresh" blood full of oxygen and nutrients to the cells in blood vessels called **arteries.** "Old" blood carrying the cell's waste materials, including carbon dioxide, travels back to the heart through blood vessels called **veins.**

Capillaries, the tiniest blood vessels, exchange materials with cells. As blood flows through capillaries, it drops off fresh materials, such as oxygen (red), and picks up waste materials, such as carbon dioxide (blue).

Capillaries Around a Cell

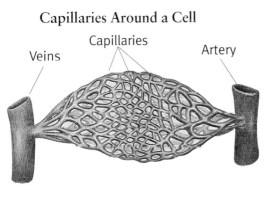

Veins

Capillaries

Artery

The blood vessels closest to the pumping organs are the largest and strongest. As they extend through the body, they branch into smaller and smaller blood vessels until they are thin **capillaries.** Materials pass between the blood and the cells through the thin capillary walls and the cell membranes.

Circulatory systems help to maintain homeostasis by changing the speed at which materials are moved through the body.

Vein

Heart

Artery

Humans have a closed circulatory system in which blood flows through a series of blood vessels. The heart pumps blood to the body in arteries (red). Blood returns to the heart in veins (blue).

A sea star has a closed circulatory system.

The Human Heart

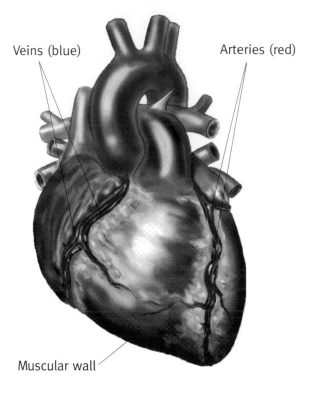

Veins (blue)

Arteries (red)

Muscular wall

The heart is a shell of thick, dense muscle tissue with four hollow chambers inside that connect to the major arteries (red) and veins (blue) in your body.

When you stand up, how does your blood get to your brain instead of pooling inside your feet? The heart pumps blood through your whole body. And it never stops pumping. If it did, your cells would stop receiving the materials they need to survive.

Your heart is nestled between your lungs inside your rib cage. It has four **chambers**, or spaces, where the blood collects— two on the right and two on the left. The upper chambers on each side are called **atria** (singular: atrium) and the lower chambers are called **ventricles**. Blood enters the heart through the atria and leaves the heart through the ventricles. The thick muscular walls of the chambers contract to make the heart "pump."

Blood always flows through your heart and your body in one direction. That way it can get rid of waste and receive a fresh supply of nutrients and oxygen before passing by the cells again. To prevent the blood from moving backward, at the entrance of each chamber, the heart has a series of **valves**, which act like automatic doors. They close once blood enters a chamber, thereby forcing it to exit in the proper direction.

Blood is pumped through the heart twice as it circulates through the body— once through the right side and once through the left. A layer of tissue separates the two sides of the heart so that the blood in each side never mixes.

Inside of Human Heart

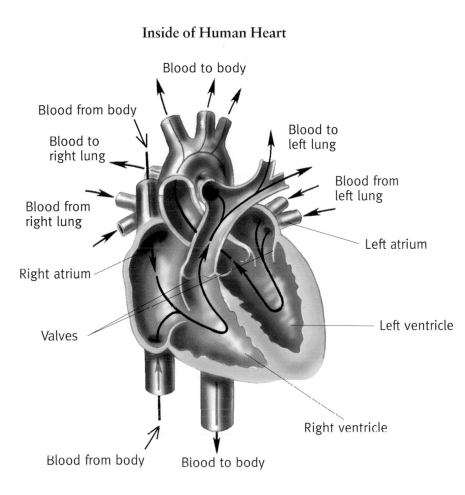

Blood to body

Blood from body

Blood to right lung

Blood from right lung

Right atrium

Valves

Blood to left lung

Blood from left lung

Left atrium

Left ventricle

Right ventricle

Blood from body

Blood to body

Blood carried by veins from the body enters the heart through the right atrium. It flows into the right ventricle and is pumped to the lungs. Blood full of oxygen from the lungs enters the left atrium. It flows into the left ventricle and is pumped into the body's arteries to be carried to the body's cells.

Blood returning from the body first enters the right atrium where it passes into the right ventricle. It is pumped out of the right ventricle and sent straight to the lungs, where it gets rid of the carbon dioxide and picks up a fresh supply of oxygen. From the lungs, the oxygen-rich blood enters the left atrium where it is sent to the left ventricle. From the left ventricle, the blood begins its circuit through the body's blood vessels again.

Heart Inside the Ribcage

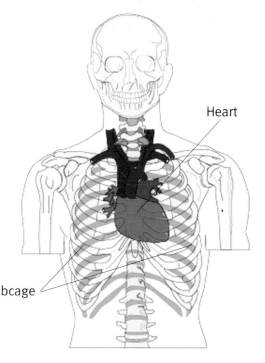

Heart

Ribcage

The Digestive System

When you eat food, you chew, swallow, and stop thinking about it. You move on and do other things. Inside your body, however, your swallowed food is just beginning a long journey through your **digestive system**. Animals cannot use the food they eat until it has been digested, or broken down into its nutrients, so the digestive systems in animals is very important.

The bodies of some animals, including jellyfish, sea stars, and octopuses, use the same opening in their bodies to take in food and get rid of waste. They have a "two-way" digestive system.

Octopuses have two-way digestive systems. They take in food and get rid of waste through their mouths.

When they eat, the food goes into a large space, called a central cavity. There the food is broken down into particles small enough to pass through the cell membranes. Once inside the cells, the food particles finish breaking down into useful nutrients. The unusable waste materials then take the reverse path that the food took. They travel out through the cell membrane and back into the central cavity, where they are pushed out the same hole through which the food came.

Ants will quickly devour the sweet foods they find, like this peanut butter and jelly sandwich.

More complex animals, including humans, have a "one-way" digestive system. Food goes in one opening, the mouth, and waste leaves the body through another opening, the anus. Between these two openings is a long series of tubes and saclike organs where the food gets digested. Once digested, the nutrients are absorbed into the bloodstream, where they travel to the body's cells.

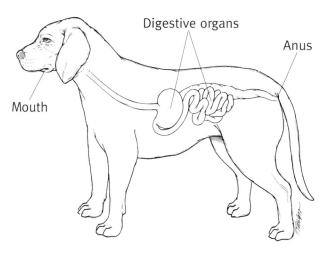

A dog has a one-way digestive system. It eats food through its mouth, but waste leaves the body through its anus.

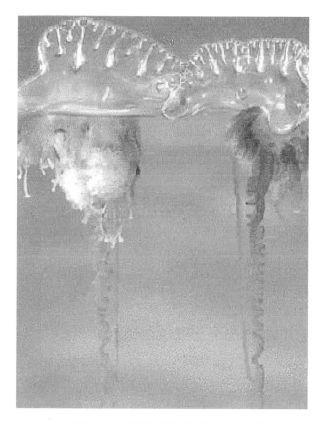

Because jellyfish bodies are clear, you can sometimes see their food being digested.

Once nutrients reach a cell, they are processed and stored by special organelles, lysosomes and (in some animals) **vacuoles**. Chemicals in these organelles break down the food particles into their most basic components, to be stored until they are needed.

Squirrels must eat a lot of nuts to get the fuel they need.

The Human Digestive System

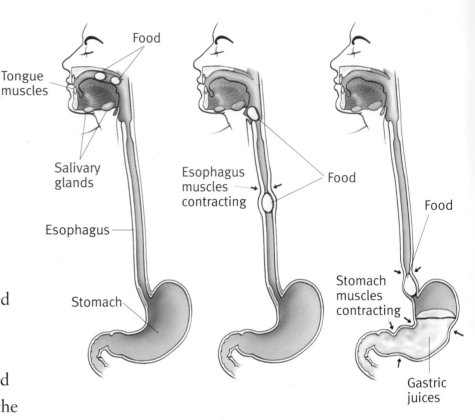

When you bite down on a sandwich, your teeth break it into smaller pieces that are easy to swallow. At the same time a liquid, called saliva (spit), rushes into your mouth. Saliva contains chemicals called **enzymes** that mix with the food and start to digest it.

Your swallowed food travels down your **esophagus,** a tube that leads to your stomach. The esophagus is surrounded by muscles that move like a wave to push the food toward your **stomach.** Because of this muscle movement, called **peristalsis,** you could eat food even if you were upside down and it would still get to your stomach.

Food spends a few hours in the stomach, where it is churned up with more enzymes and acidic "gastric juices." Eventually, it all becomes a thick soup of partially digested food and chemicals, called **chyme.** The

When you eat, the muscles in your tongue move food as you chew. Saliva from your salivary glands begins to chemically break down the food in your mouth (left). After you swallow, the muscles in your esophagus push food toward the stomach by peristalsis (middle). Once food reaches your stomach, the muscles in stomach walls contract and mix the food with gastric juices (right).

chyme enters the **small intestine,** a narrow, winding tube, where it encounters yet more digestive chemicals made by two organs, the **liver** and **pancreas.** The chemicals finish digesting the last bits of food.

A Close Look Inside the Digestive Organs

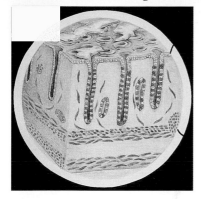

STOMACH: *Gastric juices enter the stomach through its muscular walls and continue to chemically break down food particles.*

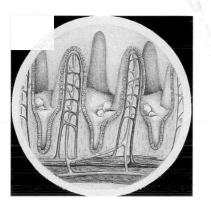

SMALL INTESTINE: *Nutrients pass through the villi, fingerlike projections on the walls of the small intestine, and enter your bloodstream.*

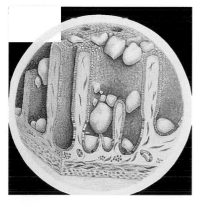

LARGE INTESTINE: *Waste materials are gathered in the large intestine before leaving the body.*

Most of your digestive organs are located in your abdomen.

Mouth

Esophagus

Large intestine

Liver

Stomach

Small intestine

Any remaining material— indigestible food, excess nutrients, and water— is passed into the **large intestine**, a wide, muscular tube. Water is absorbed from the large intestine, and the rest is stored as solid waste until it can leave the body.

Nutrients are small enough to pass through the walls of the digestive organs and into capillaries, where blood transports them to cells. Extra nutrients are stored in the liver. Some food is easily digested and passes into the blood from the mouth and stomach. Most food takes longer to digest and, therefore, most nutrients are absorbed into the blood through the walls of the small intestine.

The Excretory System
Dealing With Waste

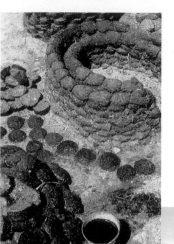

What is waste to one animal can be useful to another. Farmers use cow feces, called manure, to fertilize their fields. Manure can also be mixed with straw to create strong dung walls.

All animals produce waste. Waste is all the material that is not useful to the body, and needs to be removed.

Carbon dioxide made by cells is waste. Food that could not be digested is waste. Even some of the chemicals produced by the body become waste once they are no longer needed. Imagine if you never threw away your trash at home. It would pile up, get in the way, and start to smell. If an animal could not get rid of its body's waste, its body would not function properly.

All animals have **excretory systems** that find, gather, and remove waste from their bodies. Waste materials leave cells through the cell membrane. Then special organs and structures collect and remove it.

Solid waste, called **feces**, is usually a combination of undigested food, old cells, bacteria, water, and leftover chemicals from the digestion process. Animals with two-way digestive systems get rid of feces through the same hole through which they take in food. Animals with one-way digestive systems get rid of waste through the anus, located at the opposite end of their body from the mouth.

Waste gases are produced during respiration and digestion. Carbon dioxide leaves the body through the breathing organs and structures— lungs, gills, spiracles, and pores. Gases from digestion leave through the mouth (burping) and anus (farting).

Athletes must be careful not to lose too much water or salt from sweating.

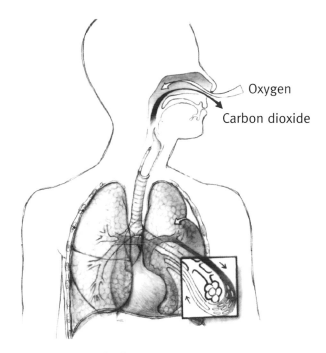

Oxygen

Carbon dioxide

When you exhale, you are getting rid of gas waste, carbon dioxide.

Waste also leaves the body through the skin of some animals. When animals **sweat**, the moisture they produce is not just water, but also contains salt and liquid waste from the body. This liquid waste, called **urea**, is made in the liver and transported in the blood. Sweating serves two purposes in many animals. It helps to control body temperature and is a way for waste to leave the body.

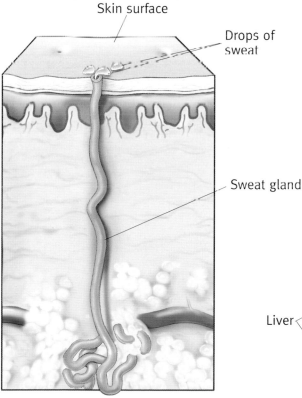

Skin surface

Drops of sweat

Sweat gland

Sweat glands beneath your skin send sweat to the skin's surface. Sweat is a combination of urea, water, and salt.

Waste materials from the blood are turned into urea in the liver.

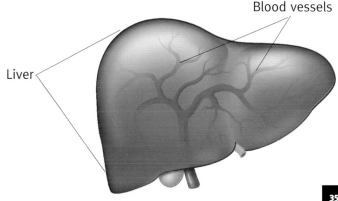

Blood vessels

Liver

The Human Urinary System

Your body has a special system of organs, called the **urinary system,** that filters waste from the blood, stores it, and gets rid of it. The blood transports urea, old cells, excess salt, and unwanted water to special organs called **kidneys.** Kidneys are the filtering machines for the blood. Humans have two kidneys located in the lower back, one on either side of the spine. They are small organs whose main purpose is to collect liquid and waste from the blood. The blood gets filtered as it passes through tiny filters called **nephrons,** in the outer layers of the kidneys. Waste and water taken from the blood then trickle down into collection chambers in the middle of the kidneys, where they are mixed. The result is a liquid waste called **urine.** Urine flows through **ureter tubes** to the be stored in the **bladder,** an expandable sac-like organ.

Kidneys filter water, salt, and urea out of the blood. The blood is filtered by tiny nephrons and waste is emptied into a collection chamber. The liquid waste, now called urine, travels to the bladder through the ureter tubes.

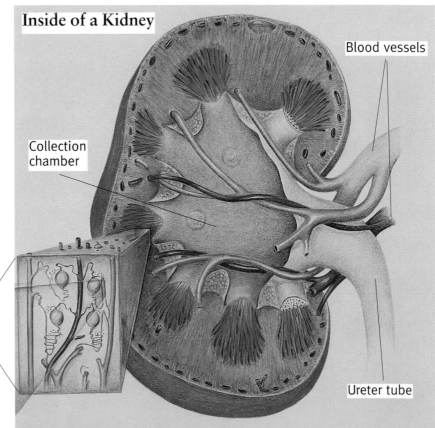

Inside of a Kidney

Blood vessels

Collection chamber

Close up of a nephron

Ureter tube

Male Urinary System

Blood vessels

Heart

Kidneys

Bladder

Ureter tubes

Urethra

The urinary system consists of the kidneys, ureter tubes, bladder, and urethra.

The human bladder can hold about a 1/2 liter of urine at one time, and humans produce about 1.5 liters of urine each day. This is why you typically have to go to the bathroom a few times a day. In fact, it is important for you to "urinate" or get rid of urine each day because the body needs to get rid of the waste in the blood.

The kidneys play an important role in homeostasis. They maintain healthy levels of salt and water in the body. If the body is low on water or salt, the nephrons can return some of the water and salt they filtered back to the blood.

If the bladder gets full, the muscles surrounding it begin to contract forcing the urine down a tube, called the **urethra,** where it can exit the body. When you "have to go to the bathroom" the discomfort you are feeling comes from the bladder muscles contracting, telling you that the bladder needs to be emptied.

Close-up of the Bladder

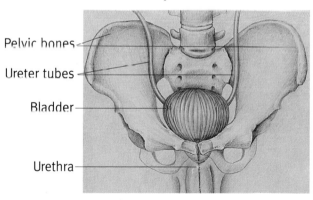

Pelvic bones

Ureter tubes

Bladder

Urethra

The bladder sits between the pelvic bones and receives urine through the ureter tubes. The bladder is surrounded by muscles that expand when the bladder is full and contract to push urine down the urethra and out of the body.

The Immune System
An Animal's Defenses

Animals' bodies are designed to protect themselves against the millions of tiny bacteria, worms, protozoa, and viruses that try to invade them every day. These substances, called **pathogens** or "germs," are what cause an animal to get sick. But they have to get through the body's defenses first. To fight pathogens, an animals uses its **immune system.** The word immune literally means "the protection against disease." **Disease** is a condition in which an animal's body systems cannot function normally.

A fluke is a tiny flatworm that infects water and causes the disease Bilharzia.

The influenza virus (above) causes "the flu."

The first line of defense against pathogens is the skin. It is the barrier between the inside of an animal and the outside world. Skin is thick, with many layers of cells. The outermost cells are woven together to help keep moisture in and pathogens out. Skin is also acidic, which is toxic to invaders.

E. coli (Escheriscis coli) is a bacteria that lives in infected meat. Meat must be cooked properly to kill E. coli.

Section of Skin

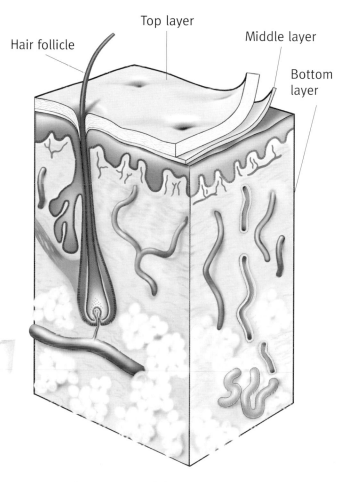

Hair follicle

Top layer

Middle layer

Bottom layer

Your skin is a tough line of defense. The top layer is dead skin cells, the middle layer is thin, and the bottom layer is very thick. Hair grows from the thick bottom layer.

Most pathogens die on the skin's surface before they can get into the body. Some pathogens, however, make it to the body's the natural openings—the mouth, eyes, nostrils, and ears. Fluids and chemicals, including saliva, tears, and even earwax, line the body's openings and kill many pathogens before they can enter the body's systems.

A turtle's tears wash germs from its eyes.

When unnatural openings occur in the skin—if it is torn or cut—the body works to close the hole as quickly as possible. Blood, mixed with a substance called **fibrin**, will collect in the hole and harden as a scab until new skin cells can be made.

Once inside, a pathogen meets a second line of defense. **White blood cells** circulate through the blood looking to pick a fight with a pathogen. When it finds a suspicious-looking germ, the white blood cell leaves the blood, and surrounds and attempts to destroy the germ.

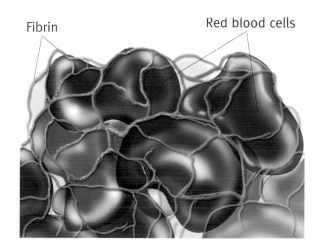

Fibrin

Red blood cells

Blood cells bind together with a substance called fibrin to create a sturdy scab.

39

The Human Immune System

Pathogen

Lymphocyte

A lymphocyte attacks a pathogen.

The human body has many kinds of white blood cells to fight disease. They are made inside your bones—in **bone marrow**—and travel in the blood. Each kind of white blood cell has a specific job in protecting your body from foreign substances. When you get sick, your bones produce extra white blood cells to increase its army of germ-fighting soldiers.

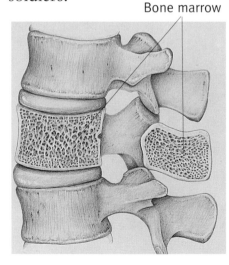

Bone marrow

White blood cells are produced in bone marrow, the living tissue inside bones.

If a pathogen makes it past the first two defenses, it tries to get inside your cells. But cell membranes recognize what is supposed to go inside the cell and do not easily let other things inside.

Sometimes, pathogens can disguise themselves so they appear to be something that the cell membrane recognizes, and they are let inside where they can cause disease.

The third and toughest defenders in your immune system are the **lymphocytes,** white blood cells with memories. When lymphocytes find a pathogen, they create **antibodies** that attach to the pathogen. Once tagged with an antibody, a pathogen cannot infect a cell and other white blood cells know to destroy it.

The body produces many kinds of white blood cells.

Lymphocytes create unique antibodies for each kind of pathogen they encounter. If the same pathogen invades the body again, the lymphocytes remember it and create the antibodies for it before it can create problems.

Despite all of your defense systems, you can still become sick. Many people take medicine to fight disease. Some medicines are designed to kill pathogens. Others help the body function properly despite the disease. **Vaccines** are preventative medicines that teach your body to produce the antibodies ahead of time for certain pathogens. Above all, healthy eating is important to keep your immune system working properly.

Lymph nodes

Lymphocytes collect in lymph nodes found mostly in your neck, armpits and pelvis. When needed, lymphocytes are sent through the bloodstream to fight infection.

Lymphocyte

Antibodies

When one lymphocyte learns to make an antibody for a pathogen, it will teach other lymphocytes to also make that antibody.

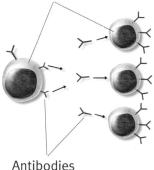

Vaccines are protection against disease.

Creating New Life
Reproduction

Animals are born, grow, and eventually die. Therefore, the most important thing they do is to **reproduce,** or create new life to take their place once they die. Animal life would not continue if it couldn't reproduce.

Pigs are mammals. Their offspring develop inside their bodies and are born live. Piglets suckle milk from their mother.

Sea anemones reproduce by dividing in two.

Some animals reproduce by division. Sea anemones stretch their bodies lengthwise and then pinch them off in the middle to create two new animals. When a flatworm reproduces, it splits off into many pieces, each of which can develop into a new worm. When an animal divides, it creates an exact copy (or copies) of itself.

There are a variety of ways that **species,** or kinds, or animals create new life, but they all have one thing in common. Each individual can only produce an animal of its own species. A sponge cannot create a worm. A fish cannot create a parrot.

Some offspring do not look like their parents at birth. A frog begins its life as a swimming tadpole.

Like all birds, a whooping crane chick develops inside an egg (top). When it is ready to hatch, it cracks through the shell (middle). A chick is born! (bottom)

For many animals that reproduce by fusion, the offspring develop in a protective case called an egg. The eggs of aquatic animals, such as fish and amphibians, are thin and soft. The eggs of land animals, such as birds and most reptiles, have a rigid shell. In most mammals, the offspring develops inside the body of the female until it is ready to be born.

Many animals, including humans, reproduce by the fusion (joining) of two cells from two different individuals. In these species there are two types, or sexes, of individuals—males and females. A male sex cell, a sperm, joins with a female sex cell, an ovum, to create the first cell of a new animal, or offspring. This cell divides in two. Then the two cells divide making four. The cells continue to divide, making different kinds of cells, tissues, and organs. The new animal is a combination of the two parents.

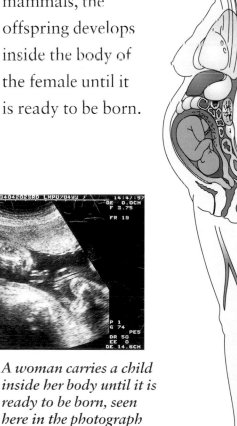

A woman carries a child inside her body until it is ready to be born, seen here in the photograph above (a sonogram) and the diagram right.

43

The Body is a Finely Tuned Machine

An animal's body systems stay in constant communication because they need to coordinate with one another to carry out certain activities.

For example, your respiratory and circulatory systems coordinate to maintain oxygen levels. When you exercise, your cells need extra oxygen for extra energy. In response, your brain tells your lungs to breathe faster. But it also has to tell your heart to pump faster. Your lungs can take extra oxygen into the body, but it is your blood that has to transport that extra oxygen to your cells. When you stop exercising, your brain tells both your lungs and heart to slow down again.

The body is a finely tuned machine, constantly adapting as it learns new skills

44

All animals need to maintain a constant supply of nutrients

Similarly, your digestive, circulatory, and endocrine systems coordinate to maintain a constant supply of nutrients to the cells. Food is broken down into nutrients in the digestive system, but it is not useful until it reaches the cells. Once food is digested, the nutrients are either transported to the cells through the blood or stored for later uses. Hormones from the endocrine system tell the blood when to increase its supply of nutrients or when to put it into storage.

Homeostasis, growth, movement, digestion, respiration, and fighting disease. Learning, remembering, adapting, and developing. Every time you look into the mirror, know that your body is extremely busy. So is the body of every other person and every animal. There are billions of animals living on Earth today. Inside each of their bodies is an intricate system of working parts constantly adjusting to changes in their lives and making sure that life itself will continue.

Zebra grazing on the Serengeti Plains, in Tanzania.

Glossary

adapt To become suitable in a new situation or environment.

alveoli Tiny air sacs in each lung through which oxygen enters and carbon dioxide leaves the blood.

animal physiology The branch of biology that deals with the internal workings of living animals.

antibody A protein that fights infection.

artery One of the blood vessels that carries blood from the heart to all the other parts of the body.

atrium One of the upper chambers of the heart that takes blood from the veins and pumps it into a ventricle.

bladder The organ where waste liquid is stored before it leaves the body.

blood The red liquid that transports materials through the body, often pumped by a heart.

blood vessel A narrow tube in the body through which blood flows.

bone marrow A soft, reddish substance inside some bones that helps produce blood cells.

brain The organ that is the controlling center of the nervous system in vertebrates.

bronchi The tubes in the lungs through which air passes.

capillary A small blood vessel that carries blood between the arteries and veins.

carbohydrate A natural substance that is an important source of energy for animals. Bread, pasta, and potatoes are all carbohydrates.

carbon dioxide A gas with no color or smell that is a mixture of carbon and oxygen. Animals breathe this gas out.

cell The basic unit of living things. There are many different types of cells, each with a different job to do.

cell membrane The outer covering of a cell. The cell membrane allows certain substances to pass through it.

central cavity A large space inside the bodies of some animals that is used to digest food and gather waste.

chamber In a human heart, one of the four spaces where blood collects.

chyme Partially digested food passed from the stomach to the small intestine.

circulatory system The body system that pumps blood around the body.

cytoplasm The jellylike matter of a living cell which is found outside the nucleus.

diaphragm A dome-shaped muscle below the lungs that assists in breathing.

digestive system The system in the body that breaks down food so that it can be absorbed into the blood.

disease An illness.

ectothermic Describes animals that can only regulate their body temperatures behaviorally.

endocrine system The network of glands that secrete hormones and regulate chemicals in the body.

endothermic Describes animals that can regulate their body temperatures both physiologically and behaviorally.

enzyme A chemical in the body that helps break food down into nutrients during digestion.

esophagus The tube that carries food from the mouth to the stomach.

excretory system The body system responsible for passing waste matter out of the body.

exoskeleton A hard protective covering on the outside of many organisms. Insects have exoskeletons.

fat A nutrient that keeps a body warm and gives it energy. Meat, nuts, and avocados are all rich in fats.

feces The body's solid waste matter.

fibrin The substance that binds with blood, making it harden into a scab.

ganglion A simple, brain-like organ found some animals. Flying insects have ganglia.

gill The breathing organ of fish and some other aquatic animals.

gland An organ that produces special chemicals called hormones.

heart The muscular organ that pumps blood around the body.

homeostasis A state of balance reached through reactions within a cell or organism.

hormone A chemical "message" produced in an endocrine gland that affects a body's growth and development.

immune system The body system that recognizes and fights diseases.

impulse A nerve or muscle signal that stimulates activity.

invertebrate An animal without a backbone. Insects and worms are examples of invertebrates.

kidney An organ in the body that removes waste matter from blood and turns it into urine.

large intestine The thick, lower end of the digestive tract where solid waste is gathered and leaves the body.

liver The large organ which helps digest food and cleans the blood.

ligament Connective tissue that holds bones together at movable joints.

lung A spongy organ inside the rib cage used for breathing.

lysosome An organelle containing powerful enzymes.

lymphocyte A kind of white blood cell that produces antibodies to fight infection.

minerals Inorganic substances that must be ingested by animals or plants in order for them to remain healthy. Foods rich in minerals include vegetables, fruit, seafood, and nuts.

mitochondria The organelle that produces energy.

motor neurons Nerve cells that deliver orders from the brain and spinal cord telling the body what to do.

muscle A body tissue that produces movement.

nephron A tiny filter in the kidney that filters water and waste from the blood.

nerve A thin fiber that sends messages between the brain or spinal cord and other parts of the body.

nerve cord A strand of nerve tissue that runs the length of the body and forms the main part of an animal's nervous system. The spinal cord is an example of a nerve cord.

nerve net A simple nervous system containing nerve cells but no brain. Some invertebrates, such as jellyfish, have nerve nets.

nervous system The network of nerve fibers in most animals that sends sensations to the brain and movement impulses to the muscles.

neurons Nerve cells that make up the nervous system and carry electrical messages through a body.

nucleus The organelle that is the central part of a cell.

nutrient Any substance that provides nourishment. Proteins, minerals, and vitamins are nutrients.

organ A complete part of a plant or animal that does a specific job. The brain and heart are both body organs.

organelle Tiny structure found in the cytoplasm of a cell.

oxygen A gas with no color or smell that is found in the air. Animals need oxygen to breathe.

pancreas A large organ lying near the stomach that secretes chemicals into the small intestine and hormones into the blood.

pathogen Something that can cause disease. Bacteria and viruses are pathogens.

peristalsis Muscle contractions that move food, waste, and other contents through tube-shaped organs in the body.

pore A tiny opening in the skin or other outer covering of an animal.

protein A nutrient that is essential to all living cells and viruses. Foods such as cheese, eggs, meat, and beans are sources of dietary protein.

reproduce To create offspring or new individuals through a sexual or asexual process.

respiratory system The network of organs in the body responsible for taking in oxygen and sending out carbon dioxide.

sensory neurons Nerve cells that gather information from the body and carry it to the brain and spinal cord.

skeleton The framework of bones and cartilage that protects and supports internal organs and provides attachment for muscles in humans and other vertebrates.

small intestine The long coiled part of the digestive tract between the stomach and large intestine.

species A group of organisms that have many characteristics in common.

spinal cord A thick cord of nerve tissue that runs from the brain of an animal down the back. The spinal cord and the brain form the nervous system.

spiracle An opening in an insects body that lets in oxygen.

stomach The muscular sac-shaped organ in the body where food is digested.

sweat The clear salty liquid that passes to the surface of the skin when somebody is hot or nervous.

tendon Tissue that connects muscle to bone.

tissue A collection of cells of the same type that work together.

trachea A tube in animals used for drawing air into the body.

urea The body's liquid waste. Urea is excreted either through sweat or urine.

ureter tube A tube through which urea is transported from the kidneys to the bladder.

urethra The tube in mammals that carries urine from the bladder out of the body.

urinary system The body system that produces, stores, and releases urine.

urine The yellowish liquid waste that is passed out of the body.

vaccine A substance containing weakened, dead, or living organisms that causes a body's immune system to fight against disease.

vacuole A storage organelle.

valve A flap in an organ that can close, preventing fluid from flowing backwards.

vein A vessel through which blood is carried back to the heart from other parts of the body.

ventricle One of the lower chambers of the heart that receives blood from the upper chambers (atria) and pumps it into the arteries.

vertebrate An animal with a backbone and well-developed brain. Mammals, birds, and fish are all vertebrates.

vitamins Nutrients in food that are essential to nutrition. Foods rich in vitamins include vegetables, fruit, grains, and eggs.

white blood cell A colorless blood cell that is part of the body's immune system. White blood cells protect the body against infection.

Index

amphibians 43
antelopes 21
ants 14, 30

bacteria 11, 34, 38
beavers 7
birds 43
bladder 36
blood 11, 21, 25, 26, 27, 28, 31, 33 35, 36, 37, 39, 40, 41, 44
brain 8, 9, 15, 18, 19, 20, 21, 28, 44
bones 14, 15, 37, 40
breathing 19, 22, 23, 24, 25, 35, 44
butterflies 6, 20

caterpillars 6, 20, 21, 23
cell 8, 9, 10, 11, 12, 14, 16, 19, 22, 26, 27, 28, 30, 31,33, 34, 38, 39, 40, 41, 43, 44
chameleons 1, 6, 20
cheetahs 1, 6, 21
clams 14, 26
cows 34

daddy longlegs 14
digestion 19, 30, 31, 32, 33, 34, 35, 44
disease 38, 39, 40, 41
dogs 12, 31

earthworms 26, 27
energy 10, 11, 44
enzymes 32
excretion (see waste)
exoskeleton 14
eye 18
fish 23, 42, 43
flatworms 22, 26, 42
frogs 42

grasshoppers 17

heart 9, 15, 18, 25, 26, 27, 28, 29, 44
homeostasis 12, 13, 16, 18, 20, 22, 27, 37, 45
hormones 20, 21, 44
hummingbirds 6

humans 6, 7, 9, 11, 13, 15, 19, 20, 23, 24, 25, 27, 31, 32, 33, 34, 35, 36, 37, 40, 41, 43, 45

insects 14, 17, 23, 26

jellyfish 17, 30, 31

kidneys 9, 36, 37

lions 25
liver 9, 32, 33, 35
lungs 9, 15, 18, 23, 24, 25, 29, 34, 35 44

mammals 42, 43
millipedes 14
moths 20, 21
mountain goats 7
muscles 8, 9, 14, 15, 18, 24, 32
musk oxen 13

nerves 16, 17, 18, 19
nutrients 11, 28, 30, 31, 32, 33, 44

octopuses 26, 30
organeelles 10, 11, 31
organs 9, 11, 12, 17, 20, 23, 26, 32, 33, 34, 36, 43

pancreas 9, 32
parrots 42
penguins 15
phylum 10
pigs 42
protozoa 38

reproduction 42, 43
reptiles 43

sea anemones 42
sea stars 14, 26, 27, 40
sheep 13
skeleton 14
skin 8, 9, 11, 35. 37, 38, 39
slugs 14
snails 14
snakes 12
sponges 17, 23, 42

tissues 9, 15, 29, 43
toads 13
turtles 39

viruses 11, 38

waste 11, 28, 30, 31, 33, 34, 35, 36, 37, 44
whooping cranes 43
wildebeests 12
wolves 24
worms 17, 38

zebras 44